Explaining
Righteousness

Ed Roebert

Sovereign World

Scripture quotations are taken from the Authorised Version
of the Bible.

British Library Cataloguing in Publication Data
Roebert, Ed
    Explaining righteousness
    1. Salvation
    I. Title
    234

    ISBN: 1-85240-060-9

Production & Printing in England for
SOVEREIGN WORLD LIMITED
P.O. Box 17, Chichester, West Sussex PO20 6YB
by Nuprint Ltd, Station Road, Harpenden, Herts AL5 4SE.

Contents

Contents

1

Turkeys And Eagles

It's been said, 'It's hard to soar like eagles when you live with turkeys!'

But, how do eagles soar and how do turkeys live?

Turkey Christians are Christians who do not enjoy the full benefits of what Jesus died on the cross to accomplish for them and as a result they struggle through life unable to win—unable to know victory.

Eagle Christians are Christians who experience what it is to be 'seated in heavenly places in Christ' and who as a result 'reign in life by One, Christ Jesus.' God's plan for each of us is that we should *'mount up with wings as eagles'* and as a result *'we will run and not be weary; we will walk and not faint.'* This is God's plan for us—for you!

To ascertain whether you are living like an eagle or a turkey, we need to pause and take the following test. Be sure to answer these questions honestly. Do not study them—rather answer them with your heart's first impression. The answers to the first nine questions are simply true or false.

Turkey or eagle test

1. A good description of a Christian is
    'A sinner saved by grace' .... T / F

2. You can sin and not know it .... T / F

3. It is normal for Christians to sin every day .... T / F

4. A bad thought is a sin .... T / F

5. It is easier for a Christian to sin than to
   do right .... T / F

6. The closer we get to Christ, the less we
   will be tempted .... T / F

7. We get closer to Christ through acts of
   righteousness .... T / F

8. Sainthood is attained by only a few
   Christians .... T / F

9. To be tempted is a sign of our sinfulness ..... T / F

10. How many sins have you committed today?
    (You may have to approximate) ..... No: _____

11. How many acts of righteousness have
    you committed today? .... No: _____

12. How righteous is Jesus on a scale of one
    to a hundred? .... _____

13. How righteous are you on a scale of one
    to a hundred? .... _____

This test appears in the excellent book, *Turkeys and Eagles*, written by Peter Lord and printed by Christian Books Publishing House, Auburn, Maine.

The story of two eagles

The story is told of a mama and papa eagle, Nata and Ramon, who built their nest on the edge of the crag, high up in the mountains. They hatched two little eaglets, Hagen a male and Selin, a female. They reared them to the point where they were almost ready to leave the nest, and as the story goes, they flew off to built another nest and in the process left their little eaglets to their own devices. The next morning the two little eaglets awoke cold and hungry. For three days they were alone in the nest. Would they die? After a long discusson they decided that they would have to jump the death-defying jump of some three hundred feet in search of food or die in the nest. Two blood-curdling screeches followed, along with the frantic flapping of wings. Then silence.

To Hagen's amazement he had made it to the ground, and amazingly so had Selin. Mama and Papa had not taught them anything about survival and so they were on their own. They did not even know that they were eagles. Behind them was a mountain range that seemed to call them. As they looked with longing eyes at these mountains, they were suddenly frightened by a strange noise coming from the forest. They lunged towards each other for protection as some strange-looking birds slowly emerged from the woods. These birds were startled to see Hagen and Selin and began cackling loudly and ran around in meaningless circles. They were turkeys.

These turkeys took them and began to care for them and teach them how to fend for themselves—how to gather turkey food. They taught the eagles how to scratch in the ground and how to strut around and how to be 'good turkeys'.

Sad to say, Hagen and Selin had, at last, been turkey-ised, and still they felt like utter failures.

To help them even further into their discouragement, one

of their turkey friends told them one day: 'You were actually hatched from *buzzard* eggs. You just happen to be born that way—there is nothing you can do about it. You were just born poor, miserable buzzards.'

Months of this drudgery passed. Nothing changed. They wondered what had become of their parents. Try as they may, they could not feel comfortable and at home. Some days were a little better, others were worse—it seemed as though they were locked into a pattern.

One day Hagen went in search of Drew, the owl. In finding him Hagen said, 'I have left the turkeys but I do not know what to do.' Drew replied, 'You do not know what to do because you do not know who you are.' This puzzled Hagen. Drew then proceeded to explain that Hagen should eat meat and that he was one of the most honoured amongst creatures. This only served to confuse Hagen further. Eventually Drew said, 'Hagen, you're not a turkey, you're not a buzzard, *you're an eagle!* You are a descendent of the greatest of birds. You belong high up in the sky.'

A thrill of glory and revelation ran up and down Hagen's mighty wings. Instinctively he knew who he was. He opened his wings to their fullest, and with one tremendous sweep, he set sail into the skies. With a screech of victory, he lifted his head, arched his wings, caught the wind, and soared towards the mountain peaks—*an eagle at last*. Never again would he be a turkey! *What are you?*

Thirteen answers

The answer to the first nine of those questions is *false*. If you answered *true* to any of those questions, you have been *turkey-ised*. If you got all nine right, don't start strutting around!

1. A good description of a Christian is a sinner saved by grace

FALSE! The Bible does not call us sinners saved by grace. No, do not use this 'low' word to describe those whom the Bible calls *saints*.

2. You can sin and not know it

FALSE! We have been taught that a bad thought is a sin and therefore we have come to believe that a Christian automatically accumulates sins every day, without knowing it. This is not the case. If you have a relationship with Christ you cannot sin without knowing it. If the Holy Spirit lives in you, He will immediately tell you if you have sinned.

3. It is normal for a Christian to sin every day

FALSE! If we believe that it is normal for a Christian to sin every day, then we will expect to sin—we will not be surprised when we do. The Bible says, *'These things write I unto you that you sin not'* (1 John 2:1). It also says, *'Whosoever is born of God does not commit sin* [Greek: does not keep on sinning]; *for his seed remaineth in him, and he cannot sin* [Greek: cannot keep on sinning], *because he is born of God'* (1 John 3:9). It is therefore *not* normal for a Christian to sin every day!

4. A bad thought is a sin

FALSE! If a bad thought is a sin, then when we are tempted, we sin. The devil is able to shoot the fiery darts of bad thoughts into our minds—he is able to knock on our front door, but it is altogether another matter as to whether or not we invite him in. But, says somebody, what about the statement of Jesus, *'Whosoever looketh on a woman to lust after her hath committed adultery with her already in his heart'*? Looking is one thing. Looking and having a thought flashed through your mind by the devil is another thing—but it is not sin until the third step is taken and you deliberately gaze on and play out the act of adultery in your mind. Let me illustrate: I walk into the bank, and the thought occurs to me, 'Wouldn't it be nice to have all that money? I could steal it if the cashier wasn't looking.' Have I committed a sin? Of course not! Bad thoughts are not sins. Bad thoughts which are *received and acted upon* are sins.

5. It is easier for a Christian to sin than to do righteousness
FALSE! Our state of mind determines the way we act. *'As a man thinketh in his heart, so is he'* (Proverbs 23:7). If your friend told you that your child had just been killed in a terrible accident, you would feel sorrow, even if he was lying to you. In other words, the message that had been conveyed to you would greatly influence you. So, too, if you are told that the Christian life is *hard* (no, impossible!) it would affect your actions and attitudes. But the fact of the matter is that it is easy for a cow to be a cow and for a bird to be a bird *and* for a Christian to be a Christian! The Christian life is easy! Jesus said, *'My commandments are not grievous'* (1 John 5:3), and Proverbs 13:15 says, *'The way of the transgressor is hard.'* It is easier for a Christian to live right than to sin.

6. The closer we get to Christ the less we are tempted
FALSE! Turkeys tell you that we need to 'get closer to Jesus'. The reality is that *He lives inside us!* I used to think that the more like Jesus I became, the less I would be tempted, but the opposite seems to be the case. It actually seems as though the more we become like Jesus, the more we become a target of the devil, but equally so, the more we are able to cope with the darts of the devil.

7. We get closer to Christ through acts of righteousness
FALSE! We all tend to think, on the days that we really do well, that God likes us better than on the days that we lose our tempers with our children or become irritable. As a result we believe that we get closer to Christ by doing good

works. That is a lie. It is impossible for us *ever* to earn God's favour. Christ, and not our actions or attitudes is our righteousness. In other words our righteousness in Christ is not dependent on our performance. The fact is that *everything we do is an act of righteousness unless we choose to sin.* Sin is a deliberate choice. If you allowed God to set you free of sin-consciousness and make you aware of righteousness, it might be the greatest thing that has ever happened to you. We do not get closer to Christ through acts of righteousness. No, we are completely righteous in Him.

8. Sainthood is attained by only a few Christians
FALSE! The church has tended to teach the following degrees of Christian life: Christian, then disciple and then saint. The Bible teaches that the moment we are born again we become saints. All Christians are saints, literally meaning holy ones, or ones who have been set apart for God. In 1 Corinthians 1:2 'called saints!' Note that the two words 'to be' are not in the original—they were put in by some turkey!

9. To be tempted is a sign of sinfulness
FALSE! Remember, Jesus was tempted, yet without sin. Temptation is certainly not a sign of sinfulness.

10. How many sins have you committed today?
11. How many acts of righteousness have you committed today?
Everything that a Christian does, except when he sins, is an act of righteousness. Unless you are specifically aware of a sin that you have committed, and the Holy Spirit is convicting you, then you are not guilty of any sin and have therefore not committed any sin. Mothers are often under condemnation. They believe that dressed-up ladies involved in 'church work' are the only women serving God, but don't realise that raising babies and changing nappies is one of the greatest acts of righteousness.

12. *How righteous is Jesus on a scale of one to a hundred?*
One hundred!

13. *How righteous are you on a scale of one to a hundred?*
One hundred!

This is *true* simply because the righteousness of Jesus is *given* (imputed and imparted) to *you*!

Do not 'turkey around' any longer! Stretch your wings and fly to the heights on the currents of God's winds of truth!

2

Our Right To Righteousness

Righteousness according to E. W. Kenyon means, 'The ability to stand in the presence of God the Father without a sense of guilt or inferiority.'

This is the greatest need on earth. Without this, people live under a cloud of *condemnation*.

To know that you are a child of God and that your sins have been washed away and that you now stand in the presence of God without a sense of guilt or inferiority and that you have the assurance of eternity in heaven with God, is a wonderful privilege. However, that assurance is often tarnished by a sense of condemnation that hinders us in our prayer lives, our witnessing and in our general lifestyles. We tend to feel as though our salvation covers us for eternity, but that it does not cover us for now. In other words, we know that we will make heaven, but our present lives on earth are the problem. Here on earth we have to battle with our old wicked carnal natures, which are times we may be able to conquer, but in reality we will only have short periods of victory. As a result we have somehow ended up with a teaching that says that everything will work out in the hereafter and therefore we should grin and bear it till Jesus comes again, and then in a moment of time He will solve all our problems and instantaneously we will be without spot—perfected in His sight.

Consequently we have rated our salvation as, 'Ten per cent *now* and ninety per cent *then*.' This of course is false and is a great discredit to the work of salvation that Jesus did for us on the cross.

Such teachings have emerged because we have failed to understand the work that Jesus did for us on the cross, and because we have been given wrong teachings and have therefore had wrong ideas about the Bible teaching on righteousness. Some of the wrong teachings that have heavily influenced our thinking and our acting include the following:

Wrong teachings that have deeply influenced us

1. Trying to obtain righteousness through the law or through good works

Man finds it very difficult to accept righteousness from Jesus as a free gift. His pride causes him rather to want to work for it. Therefore he will go to all sorts of lengths to try to be righteous. Some will give their lives in monasteries, or as hermits or as ministers, or as Sunday school teachers or as social workers or as missionaries or in many other ways, in the hope of gaining approval from God—so that they can have right standing before God. Possibly this type of thinking comes from the Old Testament where *obedience* to the *law* was essential to righteousness. But this is changed in the New Testament, which says, *'A man is not justified by the works of the law...for by the works of the law shall no flesh be justified'* (Galatians 2:16). As a matter of fact, *if* we are trying to secure our salvation by keeping the law and we happen to fail to keep it absolutely perfectly, then the Bible says that we are under the *curse*.

> *Cursed is everyone that continueth not in all things which are written in the book of the law, to do them.*
> (Galatians 3:10)

The *truth* of the matter is that, *'Christ has redeemed us from the curse of the law'* (Galatians 3:13), and that the Bible says:

> *But now the righteousness of God, without* [or apart from] *the law is manifested... the righteousness of God which is* by faith *of Jesus Christ unto all and upon all them that believe.... Therefore we conclude that a man is justified by faith* **apart from the deeds of the law.**
> (Romans 3:21,22,28)

2. Postponing the full impact of righteousness in our lives until Jesus comes again at the second coming

Unfortunately we have taken many scriptures that apply to *now* and made them apply almost exclusively to the future. Let's take a look at a few of these scriptures and in each case ask the question, 'Does it refer to *now* or to *then?*'

Romans 8:37: *'Nay, in all these things we are more than conquerors through him that loved us.'* Is this true for now or for then?

Colossians 2:10: *'And we are complete in him.'* Now or then?

Philippians 4:13: *'I can do all things through Christ who strengtheneth me.'* Now or then?

Romans 8:1: *'There is now therefore no condemnation to them that are in Christ Jesus.'* Is it for now or then?

Jude 24: *'Now unto him that is able to keep you from falling and to present* ["present" is not in the future tense in the Greek but in the past tense] *you faultless before the presence of his glory with exceeding joy.'* Now or then?

1 Corinthians 1:30: *'But of him are ye in Christ Jesus, who of God is made unto us wisdom, and righteousness, and sanctification, and redemption.'* Now or then?

2 Corinthians 3:18: *'But we all with unveiled face beholding as in a mirror the glory of the Lord, are changed into the same image from glory to glory, even as by the Spirit of the Lord.'* Does this happen now or will it only happen then?

Galatians 5:16: *'Walk in the Spirit, and ye shall not fulfill the*

15

lust of the flesh.' Is that true for *now* or will that only happen in heaven?

Ephesians 1:3,4,8,9,11: *'He has blessed us with all spiritual blessings.... He hath chosen us in him before the foundation of the world, that we should be holy and without blame before him in love.... He hath abounded towards us in all wisdom and prudence...having made known to us the mystery of his will...in whom we have obtained an inheritance.'* Is this only for us when we get to heaven or is it for us *now*? Compare this reference with Colossians 1:21–22.

Ephesians 3:19–20: *'...that you might be filled with all the fullness of God. Now unto him that is able to do exceedingly abundantly above all that we ask or think, according to the power that worketh in us...'* Is it for *now* or *then*?

Philippians 3:10: *'That I might know him, and the power of his resurrection and the fellowship of his sufferings, being made conformable unto his death.'* Is it for *now* or *then*?

Galatians 2:20: *'I am crucified with Christ: nevertheless I live; yet not I, but Christ liveth in me; and the life which I now live in the flesh I live by the faith of the Son of God, who loved me and gave himself for me.'* Can this verse be a reality in my life *now* or will I have to wait until heaven?

To this wonderful list of verses many others could be added! But, the most thrilling of all is the fact that *they all refer to now!* Yes, all these wonderful benefits are available to us *now!*

Therefore, we have in the past wrongly postponed these 'righteousness realities' to the future—to heaven! All these things are part of our present inheritance. Praise the Lord! Glory to God!

How God makes us righteous

1. Through the gospel
Romans 1:16–17: *'For I am not ashamed of the gospel of Christ: for it is the power of God unto salvation to every one that believeth; to the Jew first and also to the Greek. For therein* [that is, in the gospel] *is the righteousness of God revealed from faith to faith: as it is written, The just shall live by faith.'*

Now the gospel or the good news of Christ is that Jesus has made it possible for us to regain the righteousness that was lost by Adam. For when Adam sinned, he introduced to the human race the taint of sin that came down on the entire human race (Romans 5:12), but the good news is that Jesus has removed that taint and through paying the price for our sins on the cross has restored to us what Adam lost. As a result we can once again stand before God without a sense of guilt or inferiority.

2. By transferring our sin onto Jesus and His righteousness onto us
This is the essence of the teaching in 2 Corinthians 5:21 which says,

> *For he* [God the Father] *hath made him* [Jesus] *to be sin for us; that we might be made the righteousness of God in him.*

In other words, when we meet Jesus and place our faith in Him alone to save us, two things happen:
1. *Our sins* are transferred *onto Jesus*, and
2. *His righteousness* is transferred *onto us*.
This is the *Good News—the Gospel!*

3. Through faith
Romans 5:1: *'Therefore being justified* [declared righteous] *by faith, we have peace with God through our Lord Jesus Christ.'*

Romans 3:21–22: *'But now the righteousness of God without the law is manifested... even the righteousness of God which is by faith of Jesus Christ unto all and upon all them that believe: for there is no difference.'*

Faith here involves two things:

1. Accepting the righteousness of Jesus on ourselves because God's Word says we can and should do so.
2. Acting on that acceptance by living a life of thankfulness to Jesus.

The Bible makes it clear that God gives us his righteousness as a gift!

> *...much more they which receive abundance of grace and of the gift of righteousness shall reign in life, by one, Jesus Christ.* (Romans 5:17)

When we receive God's gift of righteousness:

Sin is forgiven... Christ's righteousness becomes ours ...condemnation is over...guilt is gone...inferiority is removed... reigning in life has begun!

Receive Christ's righteousness now!

Pray this prayer!

> Lord Jesus, I confess my sin and ask forgiveness for every sin I have ever committed. Please wash me in your precious blood. From this moment onwards I will rate my sin as having been transferred on to You Lord Jesus, and Your righteousness as having been transferred on to me. I turn my back on sin and invite You to come and live in me and control my life. With your help I intend to serve you for the rest of my life. Amen.

Signature: .... Date: ....

3

How The Bible Defines Righteousness!

A prominent place is given to the subject of *righteousness* in the Bible.

In the Old Testament the words 'righteous' and 'righteousness' occur a sum total of at least 402 times.

In the New Testament the same words plus the related word 'just', occur at least 214 times.

Thus far in our studies on righteousness, we have emphasised the fact that as our sins have been placed on Jesus, so His righteousness has been placed on us in response to repentance and faith.

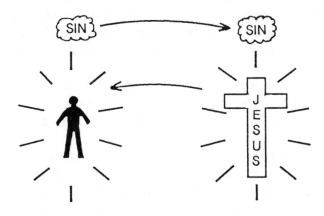

But there is a lot more to the subject of righteousness. Let us take a little time to think on some of these additional facts about righteousness.

There is a difference between righteousness imputed and righteousness imparted

Righteousness imputed

This means that the righteousness of Jesus has been 'credited to my account'. Or, in other words, I have been covered with the righteousness of Christ. Because of this, God the Father accepts me as totally righteous. He sees me perfectly righteous in Christ. Father accepts the work of Jesus on the cross as being a complete work done on my behalf and therefore He sees it as a totally sufficient basis for declaring me righteous through and in Christ.

The moment I place my faith in Christ, God the Father *imputes* the righteousness of Jesus to me.

Righteousness imparted

This means that the righteousness of Jesus that has been imputed to me does not only cover me, but it produces in me a harvest of fruit called the 'fruit of righteousness'. Here the righteousness of Jesus begins to be revealed in my life in righteous living.

In other words, Christ's imputed righteousness seeps through into every area of my life, producing *holiness* and the very character of Jesus in me. This is righteousness *imparted*!

Imputed righteousness has to do with our *salvation* and it can never be added to or improved on. It can never be tarnished or spoiled, for it is the righteousness of 'Jesus Christ the Righteous'. And what is more, the Bible says of Jesus, *'Thou art righteous, O Lord, which art and wast and shall be'* (Revelation 16:5). Nothing will ever change the righteousness of Jesus! His righteousness will last for eternity and His righteousness is imputed to all believers. *'For by one sacrifice he has perfected forever* [that is, made perfectly righteous for ever] *those who are* [literally: are being] *sanctified'* (Hebrews 10:14). In other words, through His imputed righteousness our salvation is a settled matter. Praise God! And remember, He also said that He is able to keep us from falling and to present us *faultless before the presence of His glory with exceeding joy* (Jude 24). That is righteousness imputed! It is ours by faith!

Imparted righteousness has to do with our *sanctification*. It has nothing to do with our salvation. It is the process whereby the imputed righteousness of Jesus begins to show through in a life of thankfulness, which produces in us righteous living (sanctification). This happens when we choose to yield ourselves to God as servants of righteousness. Romans 6:19 says, *'Even so now yield your members servants to righteousness unto holiness,'* and verse 22 goes on to say, *'But now being made free from sin,* [you have] *become servants to God, you have your fruit unto holiness....'*

In other words, imputed righteousness is our salvation and it is certain and sure. Imparted righteousness has to do with our sanctification and flows out of us in holiness as we agree to co-operate with God—as we yield to God.

As this process of sanctification progresses, we begin to produce:

1. The fruit of righteousness
Let us now simply read a few relevant Scripture references:

> *Being filled with the fruits of righteousness, which are by Jesus Christ, unto the glory and praise of God.*
> (Philippians 1:11)

> *For the fruit of the Spirit is in all goodness and righteousness and truth.* (Ephesians 5:9)

These verses clearly show that the seed of imputed righteousness produces fruit and that fruit is the good fruit of good living and is evidenced in the fruit of the Spirit! (Galatians 5:22–23).

Now, this fruit of the Spirit is produced in the lives of those who are prepared to receive:

2. Instruction in righteousness

Once the righteousness of Jesus has been imputed to us and as a result a desire is stirred up in us to live a righteous life, then the whole matter of being instructed in the way of righteousness comes into focus.

Imputed righteousness is received as a gift.

Imparted righteousness is a whole new way of life that needs to be lived.

If we want to learn how to live this new life, we have to give attention to the Word of God and learn all we can from its pages. It was given to us not only to tell us how to be saved, but also to tell us how to live righteous lives as saved people.

> *All Scripture is given by inspiration of God and is profitable for doctrine, for reproof, for correction, for instruction in righteousness, that the man of God may be perfect* [mature], *thoroughly furnished unto all good works.*
>
> (2 Timothy 3:16–17)

One of the instructions that the Word of God gives to us as we pursue righteousness is found in 1 Timothy 6:11–12 where three things that fit together assist us in our pursuit of righteousness. They are, *flee, follow* and *fight*:

> *But thou, O man of God, flee these things* [this obviously refers us back into the context where one of the things we should flee is 'the love of money' in v 10]

and follow after righteousness, godliness, faith, love, patience, meekness. Fight the good fight of faith....

Yes, this scripture gives us instruction in righteousness—it tells us what is involved in pursuing righteousness: fleeing, following and fighting!

Many other scriptures give us 'instruction in righteousness'.

As we follow this kind of way of life, we will be in good company, for the Lord Jesus Christ Himself loved righteousness and hated iniquity and as a result God anointed Him with the oil of gladness way beyond that of others. Hebrews 1:8–9 says:

> *But unto the Son he saith, Thy throne, O God is forever and ever; a sceptre of righteousness is the sceptre of thy kingdom. Thou hast loved righteousness, and hated iniquity; therefore God, even thy God, hath anointed thee with the oil of gladness above thy fellows.*

Scriptures like these need our careful attention! Study them! Imbibe them! Meditate on them! Live them—and you will produce a harvest of righteousness.

As a result you will know what it is to wear:

3. The armour of righteousness

In 2 Corinthians 6:7 Paul speaks about the importance of the *'ministers of God'* having on the *'armour of righteousness'*. This *'armour of righteousness'* is no doubt the same as the armour mentioned in Ephesians 6 where the *'breastplate of righteousness'* is specifically mentioned.

The Bible makes it clear that when we are dressed in this armour we are *'able to stand against the wiles of the devil'*. Verse 13 goes on to say, *'Wherefore take unto you the whole armour of God, that ye might be able to withstand in the evil day, and having done all, to stand.'*

So often, in the lives of those who are not living righteously, the devil seems to be able to find a hole in their armour and through that hole he seriously wounds them. But to those who know Christ's imputed righteousness and are endeavouring to manifest His imparted righteousness there is a very high level of victory. In actual fact, constant victory is a possibility. Read 2 Corinthians 2:14 and 1 Corinthians 15:57.

As a result we can expect to be able to:

4. Pray the prayer of the righteous
What power the prayer of the righteous has!

> *The effectual fervent prayer of a righteous man availeth much.* (James 5:16)

And we can know that one day we will wear:

5. The crown of righteousness

> *Henceforth there is laid up for me* [us] *a crown of righteousness, which the Lord, the righteous judge, shall give me at that day; and not to me only, but unto all them that love his appearing.* (2 Timothy 4:8)

4

Righteousness In Romans

(Chapters 1—5)

The theme of the letter of Paul to the Romans is righteousness!

The key statement in the letter is 'the righteousness of God' (Romans 1:17; 3:21–22).

The key to the entire letter is found in Romans 1:16–17:

> *For I am not ashamed of the gospel of Christ; for it is the power of God unto salvation to everyone that believeth; to the Jew first and also to the Greek. For in it the righteousness of God is revealed from faith to faith: as it is written, The just shall live by faith.*

The Amplified Bible says:

> *For I am not ashamed of the Gospel [good news] of Christ; for it is God's power working unto salvation [for deliverance from eternal death] to everyone who believes with a personal trust and a confident surrender and firm reliance, to the Jew first and also to the Greek. For in the Gospel a righteousness which God ascribes is revealed, both springing from faith and leading to faith—disclosed through the way of faith that arouses to more faith. As it is written, The man who through faith is just and upright shall live and shall live by faith.*

The clear implication of this scripture is that God wishes

to reveal His righteousness and that He intends to reveal it progressively with a view to our faith taking hold of it in ever-increasing degrees of understanding.

1. Our understanding and experiencing of God's righteousness is progressive

Initially the righteousness of Jesus is imputed to us. That means that we are 'covered' with His righteousness and as a result we are accepted and declared to be righteous by God the Father.

However, as we begin to understand the wonder of that righteousness of Jesus that has been 'credited to our account' as a result of placing our faith in Jesus alone to save us (read Romans 4:3 and 11b), and as we hear the repeated instructions of God's Word to begin to live a holy life, then we begin to experience the thrill of imparted righteousness.

Christ's righteousness imputed to us is perfect and permanent. Christ's righteousness imparted to us is progressive (Romans 1:17).

2. Righteousness is not natural to man

As a matter of fact, unrighteousness is common to all men. It has come down to us from Adam (Romans 5:12), and as such it has tainted and contaminated the entire human race. This is the obvious teaching of Romans 3:9–18. This God-given definition of the unrighteous and of the unconverted, is alarming to say the least:

> *As it is written, There is none righteous, no, not one: There is none that understandeth, there is none that seeketh after God. They are all gone out of the way, they are together become unprofitable; there is none that doeth good, no, not one. Their throat is an open sepulchre; with their tongues they have used deceit; the poison of wasps is under their lips; Whose mouth is full of cursings and bitterness. Their feet are swift to shed*

26

blood: Destruction and misery are in their ways; And the way of peace have they not known: There is no fear of God before their eyes.

May I remind you that this is not man's view, this is God's view of the matter. This is all the more reason why we need the gift of the righteousness of God.

3. Righteousness does not come through keeping the Old Testament law

The very next statement in Romans 3 makes this clear:

Now we know that whatever things the law says, it says to them who are under the law, that every mouth may be stopped, and all the world may become guilty before God. Therefore, by the deeds of the law there shall no flesh be justified [declared righteous] *in his sight; for by the law is the knowledge of sin.* (Romans 3:19–20)

Despite the fact that the Bible is abundantly clear on this point, many people still secretly think that they can somehow earn God's righteousness by being good—by keeping the law. Some even feel that if they commit ten sins, then ten or more good deeds will surely counteract these sins. The simple fact is that it does not. To believe that it does is to believe a lie!

Paul re-states the truth in Galatians 2:16:

Knowing that a man is not justified by the works of the law, but by the faith of Jesus Christ... for by the works of the law shall no flesh be justified.

In actual fact the only thing that comes through attempting to keep the Old Testament law is a consciousness of sin.

4. True righteousness comes from God alone—by faith!

Because God knew that man would never attain righteousness through keeping the law, He made righteousness available through another avenue:

> *But now, the righteousness of God apart from the law ... even the righteousness of God which is by faith of Jesus Christ unto all and upon all them that believe; for there is no difference. For all have sinned and come short of the glory of God, being justified freely by his grace through the redemption that is in Christ Jesus.*
> (Romans 3:21–24)

In other words, the only source of righteousness is from God Himself, through the Lord Jesus Christ.

5. God's righteousness covers us

In Romans 3:25, we find a very unusual word which is used in conjunction with the idea of receiving the righteousness of God. Paul says:

> *[Jesus Christ]—whom God hath sent forth to be a propitiation through faith in his blood, to declare his righteousness for the remission of sins. ...*

Now the Greek word which is translated as our English word 'propitiation' is used only three times in the New Testament (Romans 3:25; 1 John 2:2; 4:10).

In trying to understand the meaning of this word, we need to note that the Old Testament equivalent is usually translated as 'cover'. As you carry this meaning over into the New Testament, 'propitiation' means that God the Father has made Jesus to be a covering for us.

Now it is also interesting that the same word is used to describe the 'mercy seat' in the Old Testament tabernacle. The mercy seat was the lid that covered the ark of the

28

covenant—the lid that covered the box that contained the tablets of the law. On this mercy seat the blood of the sacrificial animal was sprinkled and as a result atonement was made for the sins of the people.

Going back to Romans 3:25, we draw our conclusion that Jesus has taken on Himself our sins and He has also covered us with His righteousness and in so doing has made atonement for our sins. In the process He has also declared that God is righteous, for God has not merely forgiven us, but He has also legally paid the price for our sins through the death of Jesus and therefore He can legitimately forgive us. Hallelujah! Consequently we can say that:

6. True righteousness demonstrates that God is both just and the justifier of those who believe in Him

Verse 26 reads: *'To declare, I say, at this time God's righteousness, that he might be just, and the justifier of him who believeth in Jesus.'*

Finally we need to note that:

7. Righteousness is imputed to us by God

This is stated at least six times in Romans chapter 4:

v 4: *'Abraham believed God and it was counted* [imputed] *unto him for righteousness.'*

v 5: *'But to him that worketh not, but believeth on Him that justifieth the ungodly, his faith is counted* [imputed] *for righteousness.'*

v 6: *'Even as David* [in Psalms] *describeth the blessedness of the man unto whom God imputeth righteousness apart from works.'*

v 9: *'...For we say that faith was reckoned to Abraham for righteousness.'*

v 10: *'How was it reckoned?...in uncircumcision* [before being circumcised].'

v 11: *'...that he might be the father of them that*

believe... *that righteousness might be imputed unto them also.'*

v 22: *'And therefore it was imputed to him for righteousness.'*

v 23: *'Now it was not written for his sake alone, that it was imputed to him.'*

v 24: *'But for us also, to whom it shall be imputed, if we believe on him that raised up Jesus our Lord from the dead.'*

Therefore, COUNTED = IMPUTED = RECKONED!

It is a 'book entry' made by God in heaven the moment we place our faith in God and in the Lord Jesus Christ.

5

The Results Of Righteousness
(Romans 5:1–11)

The moment we realise that we need to be saved from our past sinful life and that we are totally incapable of saving ourselves, we are cast on the mercy of God. Then as we confess and repent of our sin and receive the Lord Jesus into our lives as our Saviour and Lord, we are supernaturally born again into the family of God (John 1:12). When that happens, two other things take place. Our sins are transferred onto Jesus—He becomes our sinbearer and the righteousness of Jesus is transferred onto us (2 Corinthians 5:21).

As a result we stand before God just as if we had never sinned—justified!

This is exactly what Paul is talking about in Romans 5:1:

Therefore being justified by faith....

It is important to note that the word 'justified' is a word with legal overtones. In other words, it describes a person who has been brought before a judge, has faced a trial, and has been legally acquitted.

In God's books we have been legally acquitted! We have been justified by him! Hallelujah!

Any truly born again person can tell you that the day they were born again, a change came over them which is almost indescribable.

It amounts to this: *'When someone becomes a Christian, he becomes a brand new person inside. He is not the same any*

31

more. A new life has begun!' (2 Corinthians 5:17, Living Bible).

This is what it means to be justified—to be declared righteous!

Obviously many results flow from this incredible change in our lives. Some of these changes Paul lists for us in Romans 5:1–11. Let us take a look at them.

1. Peace with God

'Therefore being justified by faith we have peace with God, through our Lord Jesus Christ' (Romans 5:1).

There is no peace like the peace of forgiveness! To know that our sins have been taken away and that we have right standing with God, makes all the difference in the world. When as a boy of eighteen for the first time I knew that through the blood of Jesus all my sins were forgiven, a peace came over my life that is impossible to describe. I knew I was a child of God! I knew that if I died or if Jesus came back again, I would go to be with Him in heaven! What peace that brings!—'Peace with God'! This is the first result of righteousness.

2. Access into our total inheritance

'By whom also we have access by faith into this grace in which we stand' (Romans 5:2). Through the Lord Jesus we are not only declared righteous, but we are also given access into an inheritance that is absolutely incredible.

Picture a man who is wading into the sea. First he is ankle deep and then knee deep and finally he swims, only to be told that he has access to the entire ocean, but that is far more than he can ever fully make use of. So it is with our inheritance—it's overwhelmingly endless!

It does not take long for a new Christian, who is keen to study the Bible and to claim the promises of God, to realise that there is far more to the Christian life than merely becoming a Christian. It is almost like taking a child to

Disney World in Florida, USA. He enters the main gate and all of a sudden he is bombarded by a hundred things that he has never seen before in his entire life. He sees Donald Duck and as he turns around, there is Pluto, and suddenly an old fashioned double-decker bus that is open at the top chugs past and sounds its horn. No sooner has the bus passed when all of a sudden there looms up before him an incredible castle that is at least a hundred foot high. He stands there entranced—but the adventure has only begun. There's so much more!

So it is with the Christian life! Being born again and receiving the righteousness of Jesus merely brings us through the gateway. We've only taken the first step into a lifetime of adventure.

What awaits the child of God? Many things await the child of God! No sooner have we been born again than the Holy Spirit starts to lead us into all the truth of God (John 16:13). After giving us assurance, He shows us the truth about baptism and then about the baptism of the Holy Spirit, leading us into the excitement of the gifts of the Spirit. He then begins to bring forth the fruit of the Spirit in our lives, filling us with love, joy and peace. This adventure goes on for the rest of our lives, so long as we allow the Holy Spirit to lead us on from truth to truth and from experience to experience. It's like the diagram on the following page.

Another result of righteousness is the fact that we have:

3. Hope of the glory of God
'And rejoice in hope of the glory of God' (Romans 5:2b). This statement says several wonderful things:

1. The Christian life is a life of happiness—a life of rejoicing! The fruit of the Spirit is joy! The Christians should be the happiest people on earth. If they are enjoying the fullness of their inheritance in Christ, then they are extremely happy. Peter speaks of this joy in 1 Peter 1:8 and says the following: '[*Jesus*] *whom having not seen, you love;*

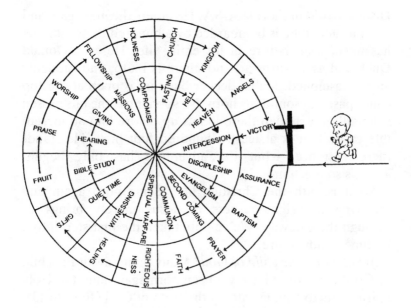

in whom, though now you see him not, yet believing, you rejoice with joy unspeakable and full of glory.'

2. The Christian life is a life of hope—in this life and in the life to come! In 1 Corinthians 15:19 Paul says, *'If in this life only we have hope in Christ, we are of all men most miserable.'* This proves that we have hope both in this life and in the life to come.

But, what hope do we have? Well, the verse goes on to say, *'hope of the glory of God!'* But, what does that mean?

Firstly, for this life it means having the glory of God on us!

But someone may object and say, 'Doesn't the Bible say that God shares His glory with nobody?' Yes, that was true until Jesus came, for Jesus said in John 17:22, *'And the glory which thou gavest me I have given them. . . .'* Then, too, there is that incredible scripture in 1 Peter 4:14 which says, *'. . . For the spirit of glory and of God resteth upon you.'* To add to the picture, 2 Corinthians 3:18 says, *'But we all with unveiled face beholding as in a mirror the glory of the Lord, are changed into the same image, from glory to glory* [Amplified Bible: from one degree of glory to another] *even as by the Spirit of the Lord.'*

In a word, for us to have the glory of God on us, is to become like Jesus. Yes, 'we rejoice in hope of the glory of God' in this life.

Secondly, in the life to come it means that we will share His eternal glory!

1 Peter 1:11 speaks about *'the glory that should follow'*. This is clearly a reference to the glory of God in heaven, as is the statement in 1 Peter 5:10 which says we have *'been called to his eternal glory'*. Daniel 12:3 paints for us a beautiful word picture:

> *And they that will be wise shall shine like the brightness of the firmament; and they that turn many to righteousness, as the stars forever and ever.*

Yes, 'we rejoice in hope of the glory of God' in this life and in the life to come!

Another result of righteousness is that we evidence:

4. Progress in our Christian lives

> *And not only so, but we glory in tribulations also, knowing that tribulation worketh patience; and patience, experience; and experience, hope; and hope maketh not ashamed, because the love of God is shed abroad in our hearts by the Holy Spirit who is given unto us.*
>
> (Romans 5:3–5)

This scripture clearly states that as a result of the Holy Spirit working in us, He takes us through important steps of progress in our Christian lives.

Step 1: Tribulations (Our testings): This refers to the

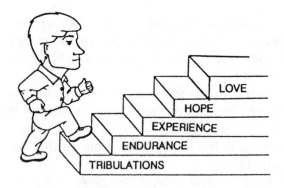

pressures, hardships and troubles of life that we all face. If we stumble and fall over this first step we will never progress to maturity. Read 1 Peter 1:6–9 and Hebrews 12:3–15. If we fail to handle these pressures correctly we will not fully enjoy the *'peaceable fruit of righteousness'*. We should rate such tests as stepping stones to greater maturity—as opportunities to grow up!

Step 2: Endurance (Our hanging in): So often Christians fail the very first test that comes their way, possibly because they were lied to and told that the Christian life is only peace, blessing and joy. However, the Bible teaches that we are also involved in spiritual warfare and need to be sure to add to our faith, endurance. Read Hebrews 6:12; 10:36. The Greek word for 'patience' is *hupomone* and means 'to remain under'. Therefore, it means that no matter what happens, we stay under God and God's Word. In other words, when things go wrong we do not give up but remain in submission to God and His Word.

Step 3: Experience (Our passing the examination successfully): This word carries with it the idea of having gone through a probation period and now having come to what the Amplified Bible calls *'maturity of character; approved faith and tried integrity'*. These are the type of Christians the Lord is looking for. They've walked the road and proved that it works. They've hung in and hung on and they've passed the test. They are the men and women of God who through God can shape the future. Nothing gets them down. But remember, it cost them something to gain that experience. It cost them pressure and endurance! It cost, but it pays!

Step 4: Hope (Our favourable and confident expectation!): Such people have placed their trust in God in the past and did not bail out when the first test came and thus chalked up fruitful experience and as a result their future is full of hope. Those who fail the tests become overwhelmed by hopelessness.

Step 5: Love (Our manifesting of the ultimate grace): This is God's love shed abroad in our hearts.

In summary, this progression in our Christian lives is nothing short of:

5. *Christ's life revealed in us and through us*

Much more being reconciled, we shall be saved by His life.

His death for us on the cross brought us eternal life! His life in us for daily living brings us abundant life! Read Galatians 1:15–16 and 2:20.

6

Righteousness Lost And
Regained

*In the beginning God created the heaven and the earth.
And God said, Let us make man in our image, after our
likeness; and let them have dominion.... So God created man in his own image, in the image of God created
he him; male and female created he them. And God
blessed them and said unto them, Be fruitful, and multi-
ply, and fill the earth and subdue it.... And God saw
everything that he had made, and, behold, it was very
good.*

(Genesis 1:1,26–28,31)

God is the Creator! He describes His own creation as
being 'very good'! Man was created by God, in His image
and likeness, that is perfect and pure!

Man was the joy of God's heart. Man was the summit of
God's creation. God and man were friends—they had fellowship with one another. The indescribable venue was the
garden of Eden. Everything was perfect!

Because man was created completely pure and absolutely
righteous he was able to enjoy direct access into the presence
of God. He could stand in the presence of God without sin,
without a sense of guilt, without a sense of unworthiness or
of inferiority. Man was as holy as God. Man was in God's
image, in God's likeness. Man and God were together in a
state of bliss; they were together in paradise. It was like

heaven on earth. This was God's original and ultimate plan for man.

Only one law

> *And the Lord God commanded the man saying, of every tree of the garden thou mayest freely eat; but of the tree of the knowledge of good and evil, thou shalt not eat of it; for in the day that thou eatest thereof, thou shalt surely die.* (Genesis 2:16–17)

They ate, they sinned; they tainted the human race

Paul takes up the story in Romans 5:12–21 and says in verse 12:

> *Wherefore, as by one man [Adam] sin entered into the world, and death by sin; and so death passed upon all men, for [inasmuch as] all have sinned.*

As a result, man was unable to stand in the presence of God any longer without a sense of guilt. Sin had entered. Condemnation had come. Guilt was a reality.

Paradise had been lost!
Romans 5:13–14, part of a section in parenthesis (brackets), Paul takes time to share a few very important facts that most are not very clear on:
Fact 1: 'For until the law sin was in the world.' This is a reference to the law of Moses, which was only given some 2,600 years after Adam.

ADAM	ABRAHAM	MOSES
*	*	*
4000 BC	2000 BC	1400 BC

In other words, despite the fact that there was as yet no law during this period, the Bible makes it clear that there was sin in the world!

Fact 2: 'But sin is not imputed when there is no law.' As the Amplified Bible states it: '*[To be sure] sin was in the world before ever the Law was given, but sin is not charged to men's account where there is no law* [to transgress].'

This seems an incredible statement! Does it mean that they were sinless? Does it mean that they sinned and got off scott free?

The answer to these questions is both no and yes.

No!—for God had not given them (all the people of the world) any specific laws whereby they were to live. Thus in their lifestyles they were not contravening any specific laws.

But then too the answer is yes!—for they did not understand that when Adam sinned, his sin had so infected him that, according to the Bible, not only was the seed of death implanted in him, but it was also passed down to the entire human race. This is clearly stated in:

Fact 3: 'Nevertheless death reigned from Adam to Moses, even over them that had not sinned after the similitude [in the same way] of Adam's transgression...'

THE CLOUD OF DEATH WAS OVER THEM ALL

ADAM · · · · · · · · · · ABRAHAM · · · · · · · · · MOSES

That was the sad story until Jesus came.

But . . . the grace of God . . . by one man, Jesus Christ

This is the happy message the flows out of Romans 5:15–21, and this message is presented by way of a list of parallels:

'For if through the offense of one (Adam) *many be dead, much more the grace of God, and the gift by grace, . . . hath abounded unto many.'*

Verse 16: *'. . . for the judgement was by one* [Adam] *to condemnation, whereas the free gift* [following] *many transgressions brings justification.'*

ADAM ———— SIN ———— CONDEMNATION
and DEATH (v 17)

JESUS ——— FREE GIFT ——— JUSTIFICATION

Verse 17: *'. . . Much more they who receive* [and keep on receiving] *abundance of grace and of the gift of righteousness shall reign in life, by one, Jesus Christ.'*

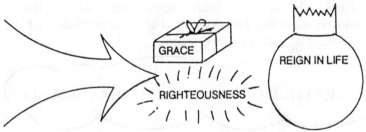

Verse 18: *'Therefore as by the offence of one* [Adam] *judgement came upon all men to condemnation; even so by the righteousness of one* [Jesus] *the free gift came upon all men unto justification of life.'*

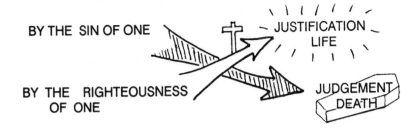

BY THE SIN OF ONE — JUSTIFICATION LIFE

BY THE RIGHTEOUSNESS OF ONE — JUDGEMENT DEATH

Verse 19: *'For as by one man's disobedience many were made sinners, so by the obedience of one shall many be made righteous.'*

DISOBEDIENCE OF ONE—ADAM → MANY MADE SINNERS
OBEDIENCE OF ONE—JESUS → MANY MADE RIGHTEOUS

Verse 20: *'Moreover the law entered that the offence might abound, but where sin abounded, grace did much more abound.'*

Driving through a stop sign may not give you an unusual pang of guilt, but if a traffic officer were to step out from the curb and stop you for this infringement, then all of a sudden the small guilt feeling would increase distinctly, your heart would pump faster, your hands would become sweaty and you would instantly be able to think up several excuses as to why you broke the law. *'The law entered that the offence may abound.'*

Verse 21: *'That as sin hath reigned unto death, even so might grace reign through righteousness unto eternal life by Jesus Christ our Lord.'*

Righteousness lost and regained! Hallelujah!

7

Instruments (Weapons) Of
Righteousness
(Romans 6:1–14)

How would you like God to use you? How would you like to
be an effective instrument in his hand?

Every truly born again person longs to be used by the
Lord. That desire in you is proof of your being a new
creature in Christ.

As a brand new Christian I was literally overtaken by a
desire to be used by the Lord, and a chorus we used to sing
in our youth meetings became my theme song:

'Let me burn out for Thee, Dear Lord!
Burn and wear out for Thee.
Don't let me rust or my life be a failure my God to Thee.
Use me and all I have dear Lord, and get me so close to
Thee,
Till I feel the throb of the great heart of God,
Until I burn out for Thee.'

How can we be instruments of righteousness unto God?

In Romans 6, a most enlightening passage of Scripture, the
Holy Spirit tells us how to be *'instruments of righteousness
unto God'* (Romans 6:13b).

Obviously, implied in being an instrument of righteousness unto God is the important matter of no longer living in

sin. This is the message of verses 1 and 2. But, how do we get to have victory over sin? How do we get to become instruments of righteousness unto God? This chapter gives us a clear answer.

1. By understanding and accepting our complete union with Jesus

Verse 3 says, *'Know ye not, that as many of us were baptised into Jesus Christ, were baptised into his death.'*

To be 'baptised into Jesus Christ' means to come into union with Him—to become one with Him; to become a born again Christian.

Paul explains it further in 1 Corinthians 12:13 where he says, *'For as by one Spirit we were all baptised into one body. . . .'* This is a reference to what takes place in our lives when we are born again and come into union with Jesus— when we become one with the Lord Jesus; when we become grafted into the body of Christ. Few Christians realise how deep this union really is. Jesus speaks about it in John 15 where He repeatedly uses the word 'abide'. He says:

v 4: *'Abide in me, and I in you.'*

v 5: *'He that abideth in me, and I in him, the same bringeth forth much fruit; for without me ye can do nothing.'*

v 6: *'If a man abide not in me, he is cast forth as a branch, and is withered; and men gather them, and cast them into the fire, and they are burned.'*

v 7: *'If ye abide in me, and my words abide in you, ye shall ask what ye will, and it shall be done unto you.'*

Jesus sees this union between us and Himself as a total union. Father sees it as a union which was in His mind and heart before the world began and therefore He sees us as eternally in union with Jesus. Ephesians 1:4 says, *'According as he* [the Father] *has chosen us* [the born again Christians] *in him* [in union with Jesus] *before the foundation of the world.'*

This means that the moment we are born again, although

we may live in the realm of time, because of our new relationship with Jesus, we are also privileged to live in the realm that Jesus lives in—the realm of eternity. In addition, Father sees us as being in Christ, not only for eternity in the future, but also from eternity in the past. That is what eternal life is all about. Consequently, Father sees us as having been in Christ when He died, when He was buried and when He rose again and ascended and took up His seat in the heavenlies. Therefore He sees us as having died with Christ, as having been buried with Christ, as having risen with Christ and as having ascended with Christ, and now as being seated in heavenly places in Christ.

Yes, He sees us in total union with Christ, from eternity in the past into eternity in the future. When we understand this, then Romans chapter 6 begins to make sense.

Through what Jesus did for us on the cross, we have made contact with God and with the eternal realm, and Father sees us as absolutely, completely and eternally united to Jesus. This makes it possible for us to be 'instruments of righteousness'.

When we accept this as an actual fact in our lives, then we graduate into spiritual maturity. Discipline your mind to accept this as total truth and then read the following verses that come partly from the Living Bible and that I have edited and personalised. Romans 6:3–11:

v 3: 'I should realise that because I have been baptised into Jesus Christ (I have become a born again Christian) I have also been baptised into his death. Therefore, when I was baptised in water, I was declaring that I was symbolically buried with him, and in the same way as Jesus rose from the dead—my baptism declared that I too rose with Christ and, as a result, I walk in newness of life.'

v 5: 'So if I have been planted together in the likeness of his death, I will also share in his resurrection.'

v 6: 'This I know, that my old life—my old nature was

47

crucified with Christ; that part of me that loves sin was crushed and fatally wounded, so that my sin-loving body is no longer under sin's control, no longer needs to be a slave of sin.'

v 7: 'For when I was deadened to sin, I was freed from all its allure and its power over me.'

v 8: 'For since my old sin-loving nature "died" with Christ, I know that I will share his new life.'

v 9: 'Christ rose from the dead and will never die again. Death no longer has any power over him.'

v 10: 'He died once for all to end sin's power, but now he lives forever in unbroken fellowship with God.'

v 11: 'So now I look on my old sin-nature as dead and unresponsive to sin, and I rate mayself as alive to God, alert to him, through Jesus Christ my Lord.'

Accepting this as a fact makes it possible for us to be instruments of righteousness unto God. Refusing to accept this as factual, lands us in unbelief and open to the attack of the devil.

As we grow in our understanding and in our acceptance of our complete union with Jesus, we are progressively being prepared to be used by the Lord.

Now as we take an even deeper look into this subject, we see that it is not only the matter of understanding our complete union with Christ that prepares us to be effective instruments (weapons) of righteousness unto God. A further dimension must be added to our lives—the dimension of availability.

2. By actually yielding ourselves to God for this purpose

Verse 13b says, '... But yield yourselves unto God, as those that are alive from the dead, and your members as instruments of righteousness unto God.'

In a word this verse says, 'make yourself available to God!'

We all long to be used by God, but unless we are actually and actively available, we will never in fact be used by God.

Testimony

Let me illustrate it from my own testimony.

When as a boy of eighteen I was converted, I had an overwhelming desire to serve the Lord. However, at the same time I was almost suffused by a feeling of total inadequacy. Had I followed that feeling of inadequacy, I would have become a 'vegetable' in the kingdom of God. But by God's grace I chose to follow the other route. I decided to be involved in everything I could do for the Lord. I went for it! Within only a few weeks I was involved in open-air ministry, in hospital ministry, in Sunday school work, in youth work, in the choir, the church prayer meeting and the church services. Any form of service I could render I was only too delighted to do. What a privilege it was to be able to serve God! I then launched a Sunday school of my own and God blessed it. Praise His name! You see, the issue was, I was available, active and involved and besides that, any form of service for the Lord that I could be involved in, was an absolute honour!

You see, the crux of the matter is that many people say they are available but they never prove that availability by action. It's somewhat like faith: many people say they have faith, but fail to prove it by exercising their faith. Availability that never gets into action is as productive as faith that is never exercised. Availability that never gets into action is in actual fact non-availability!

Then too, there is the Christian who joins a church and perhaps even goes as far as offering his help to his pastor. However, because the pastor fails to involve him or forgets to involve him he sits idle for years and thinks that he can ultimately blame his pastor for his inactivity. The fact is that he will one day personally have to give an account for his inactivity and laziness to God. Each one of us are personally responsible to respond to the call of God as He says to us— to you and me, 'Son, go work today in My vineyard.'

In what way are you demonstrating your availability to God? In what practical way are you serving God?

All of us yield ourselves to one master or another

This is the clear message of verses 16–19. Consider these principles:

1. The moment we yield ourselves to obey a person, we become the servant of that person. *'Know ye not that to whom ye yield yourselves servants to obey, his servants you are... whether of sin unto death, or of obedience unto righteousness?'* (v 16).

Who are you actively obeying: Sin? or Jesus? The one you obey is your master.

2. We were all the servants of sin. *'...ye were the servants of sin'* (v 17).

3. We (the born again) have been set free from serving sin—we have a new Master whom we are serving, Jesus, and a new goal, righteousness (v 18).

4. In the same way as we were available to sin in our past lives, so now we must make ourselves available to God to do righteousness. *'Even so now yield your members servants to righteousness unto holiness'* (v 19b).

Which master do you serve?

8

Servants Of Righteousness

In our last study we took a look at the subject of yieldedness and noted that in order to be able to become effective instruments of righteousness, we needed to settle two important things:

1. Our total oneness (identification) with the Lord Jesus in His death, burial, resurrection and reigning in the heavenlies (Romans 6:1–11).

2. Our complete yieldedness and availability to the Lord, and of our 'members' (parts of our bodies) to serve the Lord as His instruments (Romans 6:13).

Serving the right master

There are two masters whom we can serve. The choice is up to us! In actual fact we serve the one to whom we yield and whom we obey. That is the clear teaching of Scripture. Paul says in Romans 6:16:

> *His servants ye are to whom ye obey; whether of sin unto death, or of obedience unto righteousness.*

Before we consider this, we need to retrace a little and take note of a very important statement that is made in verse 14, a statement that should influence our whole idea about sin and sinning, namely:

Sin shall not have dominion over you....

This statement clearly implies that we do not have to sin! Sin need not dominate us! Victory is possible! Think this through for a while! Rejoice!

What is sin?

In the context of this section of Scripture we need to realise that the word 'sin' is seemingly used in three ways:

1. To describe the act of sinning,
2. To describe the old sinful nature, and
3. To describe the slavemaster, Satan.

It seems as though Satan is 'personified' as sin in these references. Whether this subdivision is correct or not, it nevertheless remains a truth that *'sin shall not have dominion over you!'* It is also equally true that our old natures and Satan need not have dominion over us. Praise God! We are sin conquerors!—old nature conquerors! and Satan conquerors! Hallelujah!

But, it all depends to whom or what we yield!

Yielding to Satan ends with sin. Yielding to the old nature likewise ends us in sin. However, yielding to God leads to *victory*!

The Bible says:

> *Know ye not that to whom ye yield yourselves servants to obey, his servants you are whom you obey, whether of sin unto death or of obedience unto righteousness.*

'You were...you became.'

In the next two verses, the Holy Spirit contrasts what we

52

were before our conversion, with what we became as a result of meeting the Lord and becoming children of God.

Verse 17 says, *'You were the servants of sin.'* Think for a moment on what that involves, especially if sin refers to sin, the sinful nature and to Satan. Imagine being a slave of sin, or a slave of our sinful nature, or a slave of Satan! Well, that is what God's word says we were before we were converted!

Verses 17 and 18 say several very encouraging things:

1. 'We obeyed from the heart that form of doctrine which was delivered to us'

In other words, God's Word reached our hearts and we received it and it made all the difference in the world to us. Of course, the implication is that we should be sure to continue to obey God's Word from the heart!

2. 'Being then made free from sin...' (v 18)

Quite a statement! It certainly means that we were forgiven! But could it imply more? Why, certainly! For what Jesus did for us on the cross goes far beyond forgiveness. At the cross He also conquered Satan! And, what's more, our old natures were nailed to the cross with Jesus! (Read Romans 6:6.) And in Romans 6:14 he says, *'Sin shall not have dominion over you.'* It would therefore be correct to say that the statement 'Being made free from sin' must also include the promise of victory over sin, our old sinful natures and Satan.

Have you ever really understood this statement that we have been made free from sin? That does not mean that we cannot sin! But it does mean that, through what Jesus did for us on the cross, not only is forgiveness available, but we can also enjoy victory over sin, over our old sinful natures and over Satan. This is the good news! This is the Gospel!

3. 'You became the servants of righteousness' (v 18)

In the same way in which in our past lives we served sin, our sinful natures and Satan, so now we have become the servants of righteousness, our new natures and our righteous God!

From this we can see that:

1. We are still servants—people who serve!

2. Our lives should be lives spent on righteousness.

3. We should reckon on our old evil natures being crucified with Christ (Romans 6:6) and on our new righteous natures being alive unto God, and therefore

4. On the fact that we are servants of a righteous God and consequently we are no longer under any obligation to serve Satan.

Who do you serve?

It all depends on whom you obey!

The key to becoming a servant of righteousness

'Even so now yield your members servants to righteousness unto holiness.'

Yielding involves making ourselves available—making our 'members' available to God, for Him to use to His glory. For example:

Our minds: We should control the intake into our minds. We should see to it that we do not allow the enemy to infiltrate our thinking and control us with evil thoughts or with lies and accusations.

Our eyes: Much of that which we take in, and which deeply influences us in our lifestyles, comes to us through our eyes. The Bible says that as a man thinketh in his heart, so is he, but much of what he thinks comes from what he sees. We are in a battle for our minds, and what we see and think is of great importance and should therefore be controlled.

Our ears: What we hear affects us tremendously! That is why it is so important to monitor what we hear. Scandal, criticism and negativism has a deep influence on us and can bring so much misery into our lives. Consequently we must not yield our minds, eyes and ears to Satan but to God, and in so doing become 'servants of righteousness'.

Our mouths: What we hear so often becomes what we speak, and the Bible teaches that it is what comes out of our mouths that defiles us! (Matthew 15:18). Therefore it is imperative that we control our speech as James tells us in James chapter 3. Controlling our speech involves refusing to yield our members as servants of sin and choosing to use our members as servants of righteousness unto holiness.

And so too every part of our bodies must be yielded to God, as servants of righteousness!

Second set of contrasts

In verses 20 to 23, Paul, obviously for the sake of both clarity and emphasis, restates the whole matter once again. Two statements bring this contrast into focus for us:

First statement: 'For when you were the servants of sin'
Before our conversion several things were true of us:

1. *'We were servants'*—but servants of sin (v 20);
2. *'We were free from righteousness'* (v 20);
3. Under the curse of death: *'For the end of those things is death'* (v 21); *'For the wages of sin is death'* (v 23).

Second statement: 'But now being made free, you have become servants to God'
After being converted, several wonderful things have happened to us:

1. *'Being made free from sin'* (v 22)

2. *'And become servants to God'* (v 22);

3. *'You have your fruit unto holiness'* (v 22);

4. *'And the end everlasting life... the gift of God... eternal life'* (v 22–23).

How is this possible? Through Jesus Christ our Lord!